THE *JOURNEY WITHIN*

Luna Nightwolf

NEWMAN SPRINGS PUBLISHING
320 Broad Street
Red Bank, NJ 07701

First originally published by Newman
Springs Publishing 2024

ISBN 979-8-89308-741-3 (Paperback)
ISBN 979-8-89308-742-0 (Digital)

Printed in the United States of America

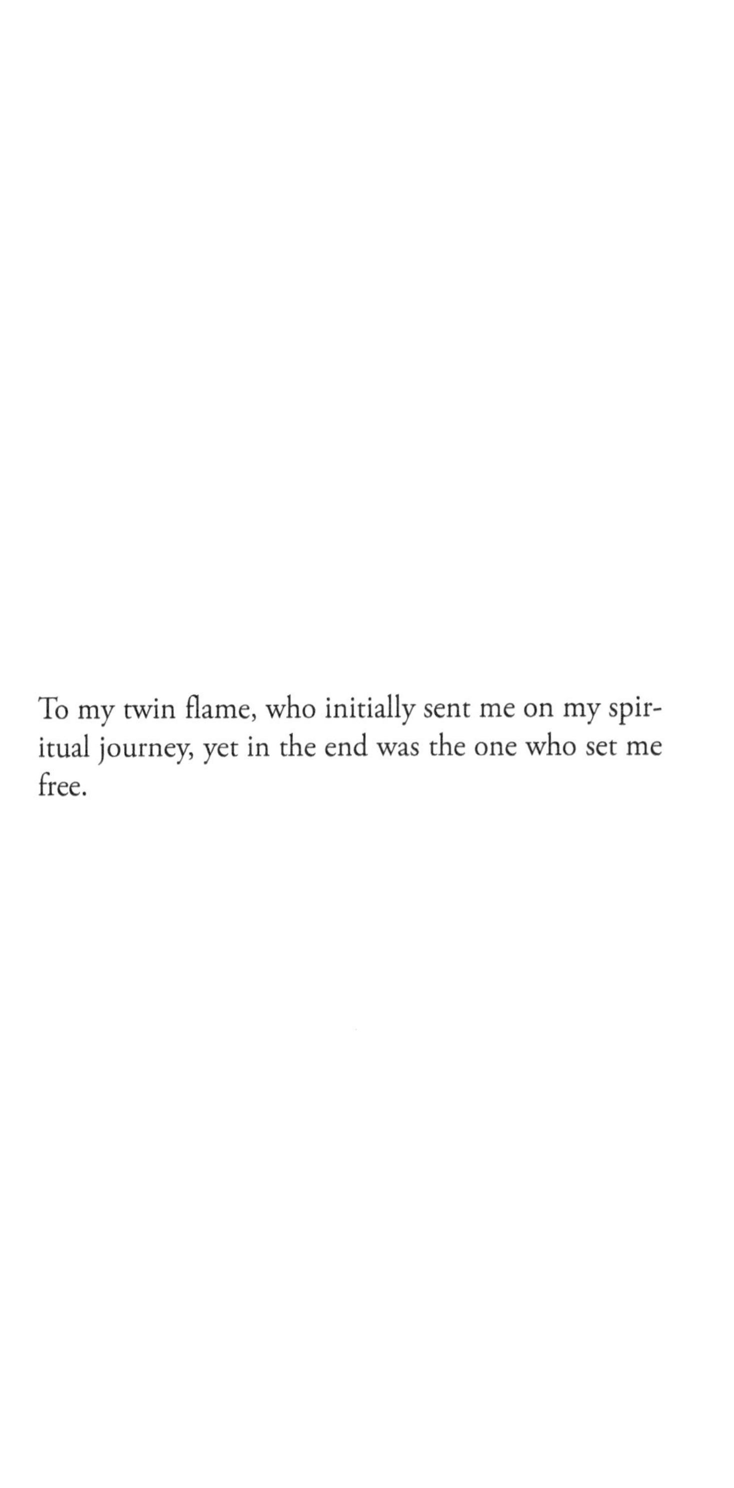

To my twin flame, who initially sent me on my spiritual journey, yet in the end was the one who set me free.

Blessed

There's beauty in the darkness only some can see
I'm one of the chosen few who have been blessed to see
There's opportunity there for you to learn and grow
Into a better version of yourself for others to get to
    know
You go in broken and come out whole
This is where you go to find your one true soul
There will be those you have to leave behind
For they no longer belong with your kind
Not everybody's made to go with you
This is where your life begins anew
It's completely different now than it was before
No more lying shattered in pieces on the cold, hard floor
It's a journey within itself you see
You'll realize what a blessing this has turned out to be
Your gifts will become stronger now
Never give in, don't ever doubt
Who you are becoming, it's beautiful indeed
These are the beginnings of the rewards you planted
    with those tiny little seeds
It's only going to get better from here on out, my child
It's a life and ride that may get a little wild
Be thankful for each day you're here, and in this new
    life, gratitude is what you'll get
A life of abundance, strength, vitality, I bet
You've been blessed from up above you'll see
I promise you this, it's happened to me

Take one day at a time for now
To take it all in, don't create any room for any doubt
The universe will bless you again and again
Be thankful for the new life it let you begin
Out of darkness, there comes light
And you, my dear, are shining so bright
The darkness did its work on you
It taught you how to blossom, and you just grew
Into this new person you are today
Be grateful for your old life has slipped away
No longer bound by the ties that bind
Blessings are yours in this moment in time
Enjoy them now for you reap what you sow
And to you, my dear, you continue to grow
Never give up, never give in
Because if you do, the darkness will come for you
    once again

Chosen One

When your life flashed before your eyes
And you thought that you had so much time
But the world came crashing at your feet
It was time for you and destiny to meet
Across the starlit sky
As your heart breaks and tears fall from your eyes
You think of all the yesterdays that have gone
And you wonder how you're going to leave the ones
    you love as your soul moves on
Will you feel the hurt they feel deep within?
Or will you feel the love that they carry with them as
    time transcends?
Time has changed a lot of things these days
But you learned to live with poise and grace
Be thankful for what you have and blessings beyond
    what can be measured in nothing more than
    time and space
It's time you ascend and take your place
Among the chosen ones in your family tree
You are where you are meant to be
One day soon you will see them again
When the clock strikes, and time once again begins
They know you love them with all you have
So rest now chosen one until you're called upon to set
    the rising sun

Darkness

Darkness swallows you whole, you can't see, there's
    no place to hide
Come, my little darling, lie down by my side
I'll be your comfort in this place so cold
I'll help you face what comes, I won't let your heart
    be cold
I know it's scary to say the least
But for now, I can help you tame the beast
You know the one, the one who told you, you can be
    whoever you want
It will do nothing for you, it'll do nothing but haunt
It'll lead you down malicious roads
It'll lead you a life full of regrets, shadows, hurts, and
    make you reap what you sowed
That's no life to lead, I promise you that
Darkness has a way of giving you pats on the back
It makes you feel recognized where you weren't before
But I promise you this, it's got one foot out the door
Darkness is envy, jealousy, and despair
It leaves you with nothing but a world full of hatred,
    not one single care
I know you want different, I see it in your eyes
It's full of make-believe, full of disguise
Now let me hold you for just a little while
Put the pieces back together, bring back that beauti-
    ful smile

You're not meant for the darkness, my dear, you're
    brimming with light
I know you know that, too, you know wrong from
    right
"Set the world on fire" is not the motto you need
Now be still, child, let me heal the wounds that bleed
Now I'll set you on the path that you need to be
The world's at your fingertips, now go be free

Death's Call

I've reached my breaking point nobody knew I had
My mind's shattered in pieces, it will never mend
It lays around like broken glass
Bloodstained pieces of a life I truly never had
As it burst into fragments like a comet sailing by
Littered by darkness no longer in light
The pieces just lay there with emptiness within
Waiting on the void to swallow them up once again
There's nothing left inside but an empty vessel full
    of pain
Even still they don't realize I've gone completely
    fucking insane
My mind's a fucking prison I can no longer escape
It has me bound in places nobody will ever find me now
I reach for what I thought I knew but turns out it's
    all make-believe
Only thing that makes sense is the visions that I see
My days are drawing near, my death not far from here
I'm walking down its corridor, soon I will enter there
People don't believe me when I tell them that it seems
But when it comes knocking, then they'll have every
    reason to believe
It comes for us all, it's something we can't escape
It's not only my destiny, but it's the wheels of fate
I've walked this earth many lifetimes to know when
    it's near

It keeps calling me sweet nothings and whispering
    in my ear
It's almost time, child, for you to come back home
Your work is almost done, your strength, your honor
    has become so profound
We honor you in this realm of magic on this very
    night
Soon, my child, you'll walk through Summerland
Where we will welcome you with open arms back
    home with us again

Fighting

Darkness takes over, it has power over me
Some days, it's hard to just be
Other days, I merely exist
The darkness is too strong I can't even resist
It took total control, what do I do now?
My voice is gone I can't even make a sound
You just don't understand the power it holds
It's strong, it's powerful, but most of all, it's bold
It doesn't care who you are or from where you came
It treats everybody it encounters the same
It poisons your mind to make you think
That things you love will always sink
It matters not to the darkness who you are
Once it takes over, it's never too far
It's with a quickness nobody understands
It's hollow, it's empty, it always demands
You tell yourself you're fine, you can get through this
    somehow
The darkness makes you question everything, and
    you doubt
The strength you had, it's completely gone
Now you're left here, all alone
Nobody knows the hell you've been through
They just think you've been experiencing the blues
If they only knew the courage it takes
To wake up and fight another day

Full-Moon Night

It's a full-moon night, and I can never sleep
When I'm within its sight, something about its energy
Buzzes around every part of me
I feel it so deeply within
To its will, I know I'll bend
I must answer its call
It's the most beautiful thing I ever saw
Never on nights like this
Have I been able to sleep, instead it's pure bliss
To feel its power over me
It's a pleasure bestowed upon me
I don't know why it affects me so
That's one thing I'd like to know
Every time it comes through the night sky
I push through, I barely get by
I run on fumes for at least three days
Because nothing ever stays the same
Everything I know changes with the moon
Everything I wish for is coming soon
It's a relationship I don't understand
But every month, I always take it by the hand
Its mystery unfolds, and I'm surprised
By the light it shines and the ties that bind
Me to it or it to me
I don't know which, it's hard to see
All I know is I'm connected somehow
I think to myself, and a small little growl comes out

There's no denying it affects me so
But in my defense, it helps me grow
It's shown me things within my path
To help obtain knowledge to help my craft
I'm better when I'm connected to the vibrations it sends
It helps me heal wounds
I couldn't otherwise mend
I'm thankful for the sleepless nights
When spirit shows me my true sight
What's to come, what to expect
In the next cycle of rebirth and death
I'm grateful for everything it provides
Just like water I'm pulled like the tide
The moon speaks volumes to me somehow
There's no mistaking it, not now
I must listen if I should know
All the things the Divine wants me to know
To move forward and walk with pride
I'll look to the moon on a full-moon night

Inner Child

Darkness starts creeping in my mind
I wonder how long it's going to stay around this time
It's a familiar touch, yet quite not the same
Makes me begin to think, this time, it has come to
      drive me completely insane
It grabs hold of me tightly, hanging on for dear life
I'm trying to pull back again, I'm not ready for the
      pain, suffering, or strife
Nope, it's locked in now, it's doing its thing
Now I hope I can just hold on to what this life brings
It's never anything good when darkness sets in
I lose myself to the void, the lifelessness within
I turn cold, heartless, that's what they say
But to me it's just another worthless day,
Pain, it seems to be my best friend
It never seems to come to an end
I suffer daily in this life of mine
I've even tried praying to the Great Divine
Does it answer prayers like it says it does?
If so, I'm ready to leave this world and dance around
      spinning wearing white satin gloves
I prefer a red dress billowing around me as I twirl
Now keep in mind, I'm just a sad little girl
My inner child cries for help all the time
Nobody hears her screams, they walk away on a dime
She reaches out to others as best as she can
But she'd rather go dance again and again

The darkness allows her to be who she must
To dance across the sky with heaven's stardust
As the red dress spins around and around
The best part of me continues to drown
Nobody cares, nobody cries
Except when you finally take your own life
They wonder what went wrong, why you didn't talk
If they'd look just look around, they'd see you reached
        out to them—they just wrote you off
So whose fault is it really that you're not here?
Whose weight is it to carry to steer?
You did all you could to reach those that you love
They didn't have time to listen to you
Now they have to talk to you from up above
The red dress and satin gloves are yours for eternity
Your inner child is happy she is finally free

It Comes When I Call

Truth of the matter is, I won't let you in
So don't ask questions, I have no answers or even
     know where to begin
You act as if you already know
The one who holds my secrets is that beautiful crow
It won't tell you anything, you're wasting your time
It's between him, me, and the Great Divine
You threaten me with darkness, that's the game you
     want to play?
Bring it on, my darling, I'll keep the wolves at bay
You think you can scare me with just your words?
Well, that's just crazy and absolutely absurd
I'll call in the darkness for you, my dear
Don't wander off, it's best if you stay here
I'll just whistle, it comes when I call
Remember, my dear, this is all your fault
The darkness came rushing in real fast
Took in the landscape washed over him at last
It took hold real tight
Poor boy couldn't even put up a good fight
The darkness took control of him
Didn't he realize it bends to my whim?
I'll let you have your fun, my love
Just be careful, treat him gently like white satin gloves
He's here to learn a lesson, you see
You don't get to threaten me
The darkness began to play with the little boy

Tossing him around like a dog's toy
Messing with his mind too
Making sure he's paying his dues
When its time was up, she said, "Release him, my dear"
The little boy was screaming so loud, so clear
The lady said, "You don't play games that you can't win
You see, the darkness comes when I call, it's a mighty
     big sin"
The little boy said, "Please forgive me for what I said"
The lady told him he's lucky he didn't end up dead
"Now run along and never forget this day
When you and darkness got the chance to play"

Karma

Karma's a bitch, this I know
She was sent here to make you learn and grow
But since you didn't learn your lessons, it's between
    you and the Great Divine
I knew she'd come knocking, it was just a matter of time
It's time for her to collect, you see
You better give her your dues
If you don't pay willingly, she'll settle up with you
She'll take everything, for nothing comes free
And give it to others and make you watch in disbelief
Karma is a grand creature, you better watch your back
She doesn't smile or frown, she doesn't give or crack
That's why you see people scrambling all about
So what about you, my love, what do you have to pay?
Positive or negative, now what do you have to say?
It's time to pay the piper, she's knocking quite loud
There's a mighty storm brewing right above your house
It doesn't look good for you, I'm sorry to say
Give good to those around, and your luck will change
    someday
For now, you have to give everything you got
Including that thing you thought you'd piss in called
    a pot
It's time to start over now, a time to start anew
I hope you learned your lessons well and your soul
    finally grew
Into who you're meant to be

It won't be long before we see
If you've still got a greedy black heart, there will be
        no turning back
Your fate will be sealed from that moment on
She will wrap you up and seal you in her red shiny sack
No more good for you, she won't even try
She'll whisper to you a sad little goodbye
See, what you give out comes back to you threefold
So give to those who need it and you'll never grow old
She loves those who think of others first more than
        she cares to admit
For now that you've paid dearly, she'll just look back
        and sit
Always watching what you do, she always keeps score
Until one day she comes knocking on your door

Life's Opportunities

Opportunities are knocking at my door
Ones I could only dream about before
So what's holding me back from taking them?
The fears I have that stem from within?
They have told me I'm not good enough for a long
    time now
Do I still believe them even wearing this crown?
The chance is there for me to take
I need to step up and take my rightful place
But the fears I have are clasping my throat
I don't want to rock the ship, I don't want to rock
    that boat
For if I do, I'll wake the darkness within
I don't know if I could handle it again
It took forever the last time to find my way out
No one could hear even me shout
The darkness takes a hold on me
And doesn't let go for what seems like eternity
It makes me quiver just thinking of the ways
It makes my life miserable and makes me misbehave
I'm not myself with the darkness inside
It takes over, and I have to bide my time
It tortures me in countless ways
It settles in my body, making itself a place to stay
Making me give up my mind, my body to it so it can
    have its fun
All I want is this to be done

I want to step into the gift that's been presented to me
But can you see why I'm hesitant? Please help me
Walk with me on this path, keep the darkness at bay
So I can enjoy this life offered to me every single day
If the darkness stays away, I'll have no more fears
And I'll only cry happy tears
This is all I ever wanted my whole life, you know—
        to be recognized for everything I helped sow
It's my rightful place on that throne with that crown
With the darkness forever, I'll never come down
But I need help to make it stay away
I hit my knees and begin to pray
To the divine for its help in this
To seal my fate with true love's eternal bliss
I promise the universe in exchange to take the dark-
        ness away
I'll continue to help people and guide them along
        their way
On their journey in this life divine
If it helps me with me living mine
It answered the call for me that beautiful day
Now I help others find their way
In this life, nothing's set in stone
You have free will to make it your own
I guide them the best I can
When it comes down to it, what I do is only worth a
        grain of sand
I wish them well and let them know I'm here
For they will always be close to me, and I'll be near
They will be part of my journey through life

For this, I am thankful and blessed instead of worried
    and strife
To each their own is what they say indeed
Now I'm in my own beautiful world the divine cre-
    ated for me

Lover's Embrace

Darkness's velvet touch brushes my skin
Lord, help me, here we go again
Its magic every time we meet
It's even sexier when we're being discreet
It touches me in ways I've never been touched before
It leaves me feeling grander than ever lying on the floor
The journeys we take underneath the night sky
Can never be replaced with a sad goodbye
You wrap me in your gentle embrace so sweet
And promise me I'm yours forever to keep
Darkness, how I love you so
You've brought back my eternal glow
You treat me with the respect I deserve
Never once knowing they threw me to the curb
Darkness, you're my love of all loves
From now till forever, you've been sent from above
To love me forever the way I'm truly meant to be
The way that you look deep into the heart of me
No one gets me like you do
Oh, but with you, look how much I grew
Into a woman who knows her desires
With a thirst that can't be quenched, burning with fire
I'll burn this town down for what they did
But I won't because darkness, you did what you did
You made me a better person than I was before
This time I will be walking among the shore
Waves cracking and birds chirping during the day

But when night falls, it's time for you, darkness, to
    take your place
Among the heavens here in the sky
For you, I will always be grateful you taught me how
    to survive

Missing You

Thunder raging, lightning divine
This is how I feel inside
The wind picks up and blows so fast
I wish I could escape from my past
Everywhere I turn, I see your face
But I know you've walked through Summerland's
    beautiful gates
Time on earth stood still when you took your last breath
Except for me, I screamed out instead
I can't believe you're not here anymore
I'll never see you walk through my front door
I know time is precious and easy to escape
But not for you, my love, my heart truly aches
I miss you so much I don't know if I'll ever get over
    this pain
I know each day you're not here I go insane
I need you now more than you know
But I get your messages sent to me by the beautiful
    crow
I know you're always with me, I feel your energy near
For that I'll always be grateful, I love you, my dear
It soothes me in the darkest moments I find myself in
But it reminds me that life always begins again
I'll never forget you, my love, I swear
For my love for you is my passion, my care
This journey we're on doesn't stop here
We just transition from one place to another

I know I'll see you again, my little brother
So go on now, have fun and play
We'll meet again on a beautiful sunny day

My Angel

Darkness reigns its power over me
"What's my choices today?" it screams at me
Do I live or do I die?
It's hard to mask these feelings I have deep inside
I feel the agony tear at my skin
It's nothing compared to what's hidden within
My heart has already turned black, you see
There's a change that happened somewhere along the
     way
This new version of me is here to stay
No more freedom, wonder, or happiness
Now it's pain, suffering, and a life full of messiness
I can't pull myself up this time
I wish I could just let my light within shine
Every time I try, it just burns out again
This time I need an angel that's been heaven-sent
It's the only way I know I'll survive this storm
And wake up again tomorrow morn

My Desire

Fate is constantly knocking on my door
Do I battle or just settle the score?
The blade in my hand yearning to cut
But my mind knows it would be too much
It's something I constantly crave, the feel of metal
    upon my skin
Just one slice would let the journey start all over again
The cool rush it gives when blood runs freely down
    my skin
Is a power that is worth it once it begins
It heightens my senses, it sets my soul free
This is yet another part of me
I struggle to deny it
I try hard not to show
My yearning's deep desire
How could you not know?
I keep it well hidden, you wouldn't know unless I
    told you
But once you know the truth, you see me like some-
    one you never knew
The blade caresses my skin softly with each flick of
    my wrist
Each cut is pure magical bliss
I know you don't understand why I am this way
Maybe you will come to see it one special day
The blood trickles down, it pools at my feet
One day I know I'll cut too deep

When that comes, and I know it will
Just know for me time stood still
For you may never understand why I do this to myself
That's okay too because time will heal you itself
The journey back and forth between what's right and
     wrong
Is a struggle I face day to day and I try to be strong
Just some days I give in, Lord knows I've tried
But it's hard, difficult to be me and deny
What's calling out my true desire
My passion, my truth, my raging fire

My Love

Darkness caresses my lips like a gentle kiss
Making promises of eternal bliss
It runs its fingers down my spine
It's grander than the great divine
As it wraps its arms around me, my waist
I lean in with fury and haste
You see, it's no stranger to me
I enjoy its company
It lets me be who I am
Without all the glitz and glam
I'm so tired of living this lie
Darkness, sing me a lullaby
Its sultry sounds fill my ears
I sway a little, I have no fear
Anyone else would run real fast
Away from it, gone at last
But it whispers sweet nothings and calls my name
There's nobody else but me to blame
I invited it in a long time ago
It sounds eerie, yes, I know
Darkness cradles me as I speak
But it gives me everything that I seek
The silence I crave is here for now
Until next time, I'm forced to take a bow
This life I live is harsh at times
Nothing but stupid rhythm and rhymes
I try to make sense of it, I swear that I do

It's like nothing I think gives me a clue
It's forced upon me for their own sake
Fame and fortune is not mine to make
But I fake it every single day for you
This love I have now turned dark and blue
But my darkness is here to carry me away
And this time, I will come out and play

Playdate

My darkness wants to play with yours
Problem is yours will be screaming "More, more,
    more"
It's addictive, I promise you that
Wait, you'll see, it'll have you purring like a cat
My darkness is addictive, it's plain to see
Yet it's pure hell, please, don't bother me
I know your darkness is knocking at my door
Begging, pleading, yearning for more
I tried to warn you, yes, I did
Now it's your broken heart that you're gonna have
    to mend
You see, my darkness doesn't stick around for long
She loves to sing nature's lullaby's song
She's here one minute then she's gone
Now look, you lonely poor boy, you're all alone
She tried to warn you about her darkness that day
When you begged hers to come out to play
She overcomes it quite often, if you will
Now it's up to you, my dear, to try to do the same
Maybe your darkness will meet again on some other
    dreary day
But should you stumble upon her in her happy
    moments, please
Don't mention the darkness, I'm begging on my knees
She's too young to face the things she goes through
    when she's there

And all I can do is watch from that old rocking chair
I love my baby so much, you see
I'll give heaven or hell before I let someone purposely
    let her darkness go free
This is your warning, I'll give it to you this one time
I hope you proceed with caution, 'cause if not, you
    no longer have any time
You can't take her back with you, no matter how hard
    you try
Because I will lay down my life for her, I will let her
    live and I will die
Her soul's too beautiful, you see how it glows
She's got plenty of beautiful memories to spread and
    sow
She's my baby girl, she's special, there's no doubt
For her, I'd do anything, I'd move heaven and hell for
    her, please, have no doubt
She's special, you see
She don't know it yet
I can't let your darkness have her just yet
The darkness will taint her beautiful, majestic wings
Then we will never truly hear how her voice sounds
    when she begins to sing
She's got a special gift, that girl, she doesn't even know
It'll come in time, she's just got to grow
Into the woman she is meant to be
So, darkness, stand down and leave her be
I command you, go away now and leave her alone
So she can take her rightful place on life's golden throne

Suicide's Dance

The darkness is there, it dances upon my skin
The silence is screaming, yearning within
My heart is quivering, bursting to get out
My voice is nothing, won't even shout
It's so hard to deal on these days
Especially when my shadow wants to come out to play
It pulls and tugs on my heart's true desire
All it does is add fuel to the fire
They whisper so softly, tempting me with their words
To most it's absolutely absurd
To those who know me it's a constant battle I face
What do you do on those dreary days?
Do you give in and give them what they want?
Or stand strong and battle and continue to fight this
    fight strong?
I'm getting tired, it's long overdue
I'm waiting for the universe to hand me my cue
Today is a day I will stand and fight
It doesn't matter if it takes all damn night
I won't give in to the soft whispers they say
I will live to face yet another day
Tomorrow may be a different story I won't live to tell
But that's the thing when you come from hell
You get to decide what it is you'll do, you see
Today is the day that I'll choose me
The battle will rage on, it'll never stop
I won't give in, I'll fight till I drop

I'm stronger than you think, you see
I learned a lot about what it means to be free
I chose what happens now, don't you know
This is my life. I've reaped what I've sowed
The battle is worth it, I'll continue to try
No more tears will fall from my eyes
I've made my decision, I knew it from the start
I just had to believe it, straight from my heart
The world's a beautiful place if you look around
For now, at least, I'm standing back on solid ground
The world is my anchor, so deep it runs
Tomorrow I look forward to the rising of the sun

Suicide's Kiss

Why does it have to feel like this?
Why does it have to be like this?
Why does everything have to go this way?
These are the questions I ask myself every single day
No one knows the pain I feel
No one knows what goes on inside my mind or what
     I see that's real
There's times I cry, there's times I scream
There's times I don't even know what it even means
The thoughts that bounce around in my head
Suffocate me, I wish I was dead
The reality of it is, this day in this life
Is a day I get pissed, things that should make me
     smile make me cry instead
This is some of what goes on in my head
The sun is shining, but it's never been so dark
The light has faded, not even a spark
To light my way back from a place that I don't belong
Yet my heart cries out in song
Save me, please, I don't understand
I don't deserve this, I plead
But words just echo out on the water, out to the sea
No one can hear me, it falls on deaf ears
All I see around me is my own worst fears
I stumble, I crawl, I climb up, yet I fall
The days turn to night, it's an eerie sound, a lone-
     some call

My voice whispers, yet my soul is bound
It hurts just a little, yet that's not enough
Slash it open deep so you can feel the rush
The power, the call, the endless night sky
As I watch from above as you take your last step and fall
The end is near, be not afraid
For we will meet again on a beautiful day
No clouds in the sky
I hold on to you
As I whisper goodbye
May luck be yours too

Taking Back My Power

I've known darkness all too well
Most of my life has been a living hell
Never could understand
Why it happened to me
Until one day I broke
The chains were finally free
It took years to see my value and worth
You see, my whole life I thought I was cursed
Turns out people played me like a fool
Many times over, I let them because I thought that's
    what love was
Love isn't conditional, you see
I learned the hard way and turned to the powers that be
They showed self-love, and everything changed
I created boundaries, habits instead of reckless ways
I tuned into my heart's desire
And within it, I found a raging fire
Something so hot that it would burn you if you got
    too close
It's only meant for those that it has chose
Those are my people—my soul tribe, if you will
I walked away from everything toxic in my life
Anything that caused me harm, pain, and strife
What I found was a peace so calm
Now my soul shines with the utmost powers of beyond
You see, this light that shines through me today
Didn't come easily, nor did it come free

It took a lot of hurt, a lot of lessons to learn my truth
I am worthy, I am valued, I am loved beyond what
        you could ever offer me
It's the undying truth
Yes, you were part of my story, but a lesson indeed
You needed me more than you ever believed
You see, you drained my light, and with it, you took
        everything I loved
And locked it behind a door
But now that I figured out what must be done
You no longer have the power to make me come
        undone
I stand in my power, no one can take it from me again
No human, no spirit, not a demon nor fiend
I am who I am, and I am proud to say
Without you doing the things you did, I would not
        be the person I am today
I would have not found who I truly am
To be able to stand firm in my beliefs at all
So I can say thank you for treating me like shit and all
But because you fucked with a chosen one
Your life will be nothing but shit
You see, I'm divinely protected, you'll see that in time
Spirit don't like ugly, and you messed with the divine
It has cost you everything you had
Now it's time, it's only beginning to collect
Your life will never be the same from here on out
For a chosen one is not something you can get away
        from without a doubt
Learn your lessons and learn them well

Karma's a bitch and now she's here for you to pay
	your bill
Sealed with a kiss, she's handled the deal

The Battle

Darkness and light
What's wrong? What's right?
Can't you see?
I'm torn in between.
Should I stay? Should I go?
Hell, if I know
The darkness pulls me here
The light pulls me there
I can't be every-damn-where
The darkness grabs hold of me tight
The light shows me what's right
The darkness drives me insane
The light knows where to place the blame
The shadows it casts dance upon the wall
Both of them waiting for me to fall
Which one to choose tonight, I must decide
I must hurry, I'm running out of time
This battle that I fight is one I must win
I won't do this dance again and again
The darkness waits for its answer by calling me near
The light whispers, "What will it be my dear?"
I must make a choice, but what do I choose?
I step into the light, I have nothing to lose
The darkness is angry, it's lost this fight
The light shouts with joy in sheer delight
I made the best choice by far, it seems

My face is always lit up shiny, so bright it gleams
I'm happy now more so than before
There's no more darkness knocking at my door

The Beast Inside

I lie awake at night wondering why I can't sleep
Thoughts running through my head, emotional yet
    deep
Trying to figure out what might go wrong
All I know deep inside is I must remain strong
It's been one of those days my emotions have run wild
I've noticed, little girl; I've not ignored you, my child
You'll have days like this, I promise they'll go by fast
You won't be stuck again no matter the forecast
It's just spirit testing my will
Will I push through or break my deal?
Today has been most trying, to say the least
I've spent all day trying to not open the gates to the
    long dormant beast
You see, if you wake it, it might just decide
To come strutting through the crowd, forget trying
    to hide
It's hot and wild and breathtaking to see
When this monster deep inside comes spilling out
    of me
It wreaks havoc everywhere that it goes
It doesn't come gently but throws heavy blows
To whomever it sees within its path
Nothing is safe, nothing will last
So let's try to keep the beast tame at least for now
And let it stay sleeping, not making a sound
I'm not ready for all that it brings

I'd like to wake up and hear the birds that sing
So instead, I'll take this one day at a time
Even though my emotions are a roller-coaster ride
They're that way for a reason, I know that for sure
It's time for me to open a new door

The Choice

Time stands still, nothing remains
Of the girl I was just yesterday
Everything I had I'd only dreamed about
Today I only want to scream and shout
"Why does this always happen to me?" I scream
This doesn't make sense, it's hard to believe
One day, things are good
The next day, you're completely misunderstood
That's the way the darkness works
Give everything to everyone, including your shirt
It's never good enough it seems
You can shine everything up until it gleams
They should be thankful for all that you do
But no, now you're stuck like fuckin' glue
You can't escape, no matter how hard you try
Your only wish is to say goodbye
The darkness makes it hard to stay
When all you want to do is just run away
The darkness has plans for you, that much you know
So you reach out to it, grasping as you go
The darkness twirls around me now, spiraling in
     waves as it grows
I look in disbelief as it's putting on its show
It's so enticing, watching it as it dances its dance
It reaches out to me now, this is my chance
I step into its arms this time
I've never felt this way before

As I walked through darkness's beautiful, decorated
    door
It welcomed me so gently I didn't understand
Why it chose me that day to gently take its hand
We've been on a journey now for quite some time
I've quite enjoyed dancing to its rhythm and rhyme
I don't want to go back to the way it was before
I walked through darkness's beautiful, elegant door

The Chosen One

Darkness all around me, that's all I can see
Not in front or behind me, I reach out for you, you're
    nowhere to be found
I scream no words, it's silence, nothing makes a sound
My heart skips a beat knowing you're not there
I look around me, I don't recognize anything
    anywhere
Where am I? Thoughts run through my head
Did I finally die and make it to Summerland?
If this is where I am, where is everybody at?
No, this place where I am, I wouldn't call it that
Is this where lost souls go when they go astray?
If it is, then I've clearly lost my way
For that I don't belong, that much I know
My soul has grown weary and is beginning to lose
    its glow
I'm a chosen one, and I can't let that be
This place is not for souls, for people like me
I must find the light, it's the only chance I got
The light's within it, it'll guide me to the sacred spot
The door I must enter to cross into the light
To regain my resilience, my strength, my sight
It won't be long now, I'll pass spirit's test
I'll come out stronger, eager to do my best
The shadows may play with my body and soul
But I'm a chosen one, I'm honorable, prideful, and bold
You can't take away my power, you can try if you must

Just remember who I am when karma arrives driving
    the bus
You'll pay for everything you did to me, she'll make
    sure that you do
My life will start over, begin again, become new

The Girl I Used to Be

Listen, child, what do you hear?
Do you feel it now as it draws near?
The power it holds pulsating within
Reaches out to you, brushing your skin
Listen, child, don't make a sound
What does it want with you? I ask
The horse's hooves pounding away real fast
It's gaining on us faster now
It's bold, it's huge, I'm in awestruck, wow
It's majestic in kind, there's no doubt
But it's clear to see it sought you out
Go see what it wants, no need to be scared
I turn to the Divine and whisper a prayer
I walk tall as the carriage came to a halt
I couldn't help but think this was all my damn fault
Its destiny caught up with me
The door swings open, and what do I see?
The picture-perfect memory of who I used to be
I'm no longer that girl who showed up just now
I stand firm with my feet planted on the ground
What did she want? Couldn't she just go?
I've learned so much already, I've continued to grow
I told her she wasn't welcome she must leave this place
For the memories she carries were no longer safe
She cried and she pleaded with me for just one more
        day
I told her she wasn't welcome and couldn't stay

I no longer knew her, she must hurry and go
Before the wind picked up and the storm started to blow
It's starting to rain, washing away things from the past
She must hurry now if she even wanted to try and last
She was a little too late when she opened the carriage
     door
A huge bolt of lightning struck and landed on the floor
The heavens fell open, and the rain fell fast
The girl I used to be is no more at last
You see, she died that day, just like I told her I she would
Now she's lost forever, now she's gone for good
That's okay though because I'm better off without her
I've stepped into what's mine, I've stepped into my
     power
I'm finally whole again, finally at peace
I've finally found what's truly meant for me

The Innocent

I love thunderstorms
Thunder clashing
Lightning flashing
Nature screaming
Or is it me dreaming?
The darkness on the outside
Matches the darkness on the inside
It lets me know that even nature needs to scream
     sometimes
So I can finally let out a final scream from inside
This kind of weather matches who I am
Sometimes I wish I'd get lost and never be found
This darkness is something I live with every damn day
But I love it when nature syncs up with me in every
     single way
It comes out more often than it should
I wish there were more ways to hide it than they said
     that I could
Darkness consumes me more days than not
I have to figure out a way to make this shit stop
It's tearing me to pieces
It's ripping at my skin
Problem is I have no fucking clue where to begin
They say talk to someone, that's easier said than done
I see it now, let me tell you how my story begun
It all started out when I was a kid
And that good-for-nothing asshole did what he did

He took the love of my life away from me
And still to this day he gets to walk free
He shows no remorse for what he did
They told him it was okay because he too was a kid
You can't take someone else's life
And live yours without strife
I don't know how he does it day after day
If I did what he did, I'd never be the same
Each person's different—that I do believe
But he took my innocent brother away from me
How is that fair to him or to me?
It's not fair to anyone now, don't you see?
That's when darkness became my friend, and I truly
    understood
What it meant to be completely misunderstood
Nobody helped me see the light
Oh, how I tried to pull myself back up to reach for
    the light
I never could quite reach it, no matter how hard I tried
So I'd sit in my room, and all I did was cry
Everyone overlooked me, they forgot about me it seems
Still to this day, I can ever live up to their hopes and
    their dreams
I'm just a lost little girl with no direction to go
Deep inside my heart, I started telling people no
I stood up for myself, and they called me names
    behind my back
Said I was addicted to drugs, but I've never done any-
    thing, not even crack
I push myself forward every single day
To make my life better in numerous ways

I will be successful one day, I know
But today I must work hard and continue to put on
    this show
As the years have gone by since that dreadful day
My life was changed in an utmost dreadful way
I move forward to make my brother proud
When I become who I'm supposed to be, I know I'll
    see him in the crowd
Until that day comes, I'll continue pushing hard
And live my life with what was dealt to me with these
    stupid cards
I'll draw all four aces one day, you'll see
Then nobody in this life will recognize who I used
    to be

The Missing Link

We knew little that day, God was going to call your
    name
In life, we loved you dearly; in death, we do the same
It broke our hearts to lose you, but you did not go alone
For part of us went with you the day God called you
    home
You left us beautiful memories; your love is still our
    guide
And although we cannot see you, you are always at
    our side
Our family chain is broken, and nothing is the same
But as God calls us one by one, the chain will link
    again

The Monsters

The darkness draws me in
Curiosity makes me stay
The little girl in me wants to come out and play
She thinks it's safe, but I know it's not
But I'll give her one tiny little shot
She runs in arms wide open
This is my way of coping
She made friends with the monsters she met
Now they all owe her, they're all in her debt
You see she doesn't play the game like the others
She learned a long time ago from her mother
To strike fast and take names
Then they have only themselves to blame
It's not your fault they fell victim to their cause
But you're the one who's holding up the fucking walls
You let go, they all fall down
They all scream inside till there's no more sound
Who would win that battle in the end?
The little girl or the monsters she made her friends?

The Trickster

Darkness washes over me
It's such a sight to see
I barely make a sound
This is how it is for me
When I don't just let things be
I had to go try to save you too
From the darkness that rang all too true
There's no escaping it now
It's turned its head, it's come back around
It saw me trying to save you, but it was clear to see
It wasn't you it wanted, clearly it was me
It took its time in waiting to strike
Then took me in and held me tight
It won't let go its grasp on me
It won't set me free
I pray for help from the Great Divine
I whisper, "Please just give me a sign
That you hear the prayers I plea
Each night before I go to sleep
I try to keep my faith
But this darkness has done nothing but take
Everything from me
I promise I'm yours for eternity
Just make it let go now, please?
Make it stop, make it seize
This darkness is no place to be
Let me go, set me free

I don't want to dance with it
I don't like it, not one bit
Clearly, it's not made for me
Can you hear me? Can't you see?"
The darkness starts to clear away some
Peeking through, I see the rising sun
I owe thanks to the Great Divine
For answering my prayers at just the right time
I was about to go insane
If I had to live in darkness yet another day
My path lays before me now
I know what I must do, I must put on my crown
Live each day as if it's the last
And never look back into the past
There's nothing there left for me
My future's bright, I am free
To do the things I must
From my heart, not from lust
The power I feel deep inside
It's grander than the rising tide
Let me follow the Divine's big plan
Because our lives are just like grains of sand
Here today, gone tomorrow
I will no longer live in sorrow
Happiness is here at last
I'll move forward and never look back
Darkness taught me my lesson well
It's time to fly, time to sail
This I must do

I suggest it for you too
Be grateful for the things you have
For darkness can always take them back

The Wings of a Dove

Darkness swallows me whole, I don't know what to do
The choice comes down to either me or you
Which way is up or down, this I no longer know
There has to be a way to break free from these mind
     games that you play
You see, I can't trust nothing that you say
You tell me that you love me
Yet you don't show me in any kind of way
The sky could be falling, and I used to be willing to stay
It's time for me to take the first step and finally walk
     away
To finish my path to happiness, the truth, my way
It's hard to say goodbye to someone you dearly love
You have to let go of what used to be and learn to fly
     on the wings of a dove
If it was true love, they will change their hateful ways
And come to realize the things they did to you and
     the hurt they caused in every single way
As time passes by, they will truly see you shine
No more ropes, no more ties that bind
Learn to stand in your power because that's where
     you belong
Learn to sing and dance to life's beautiful song
You were never meant to be a servant
It's between you and God, now you've learned to be
     observant
You take it day by day, and value what you have

No more are the darkest days that made you com-
    pletely, utterly sad
You dance upon the wings of an angel for those who
    love to see you smile because you're truly a gift
    from above
And when they think of you flying, it's on the wings
    of a dove

Tormented Soul

Nothing but torment, sorrow, tears, and strife
All I can do is sit here and stare because all of my
  options seem so far away
Out there, things play like a broken record over and
  over again
I wish I knew how to start this life over again
The things I'd do different, the things I'd do right
Would not put me on this path of pain and strife
It's like a windowless prison you can't see out, it's only
  darkness; you can't even hear the screams with-
  out the fright
That I feel as I walk alone, for this life of mine has
  gone all wrong
The pain I feel as it tears me inside
Caresses my heart but cuts like a blade
The burning I feel as it pierces my heart
It's only the beginning; it's only the start
As I feel the blood rush, trickle down my skin
I feel its power, the rush it sends
Washes over me like a gentle breath
This is not the beginning
But the ending of death
For I have fought this battle for far too long
I wish I knew just where I belong
Is it here or there or even in my own skin?
I wish I knew so we can just begin
The torment I feel is screaming to get out

But I can't find my voice; I can't scream or shout
This feeling I'm drowning is nothing new
For I forsake thee and land in a land of blue
The darkness spins me on this very night
Whispering secrets that I crave so I take flight
To fly away on the wings of a dove
To fit the part like a white satin glove
The beauty you see is only skin-deep
For what's underneath is what's buried deep
A soul so beautiful that you'll never know
The story of how her love never grows
She's exhausted from acting a saint
She opens the door
To hell's beautiful gate
I have arrived at my final place
They shout and cheer, and welcome her with grace
She's finally home now, you see
Not even your love could ever save me

When Darkness Comes to Stay

The woman I once was, I am no more
I took one last look and closed that door
You see things happen to people all the time
I can only guess
Whatever happened to mine
One day she was okay, laughing, smiling free as can be
Then she's crying, shaking, screaming, violently
Something inside her snapped like a pen
I listened to her stories to see how she's been
It took a long time for her to make sense
But it cost her dearly, every expense
She said the darkness beckoned her to come to its call
Then one day it shoved her up against the wall
Faced with fear, she didn't know what to do
So she went into hiding—hell, nobody knew
We noticed she wasn't around that much
We just thought she was staying gone too much
Little did we know the darkness had taken over her
She whispered, "Please help me, sir"
He didn't understand what she had meant
So he shrugged it off as some weird event
The darkness is full force now, can't you see?
There's nothing left of her or who she used to be
She sits quietly, hands in her lap
All she has with her is a gray alley cat
When she went missing, all alarms went off

Nothing left unturned, not even with her boss
Nobody had seen or heard from her in weeks
When we finally found her, she acted strange and meek
We sought the help of a doctor to get his advice
He didn't leave our house until after midnight
The doctor said, "She's traumatized real bad"
"What can do this to her to make her so sad?"
He answered, "The darkness got to her before any-
        one could know
Now it's up to all of you to ease life's biggest blows
Be careful around her, she's quite fragile, if you recall
This beats anything I've ever saw"
The darkness has never left her, it's been years to this day
There's not a day that goes by that I don't hit my
        knees and pray
"Please let her overcome this and become who she was
I believe you can guide her with your everlasting love
Make her remember all the happy times she had
Before the darkness came in and made her extremely
        weak and sad
Divine Source, I believe you can do this for us all
Bring her back to life once and for all
I'd love to see her smile again just one more time
And see her face light up and her eyes begin to shine
A little bit of difference tomorrow might bring
I'd shout from the rooftops, dance and sing
Let her be who I know she is deep down in her mind
Take the darkness away, no longer let it bind"
She made a slight giggle from across the room
I ran as fast as I could, my body nearly flew
She smiled at me then and whispered hello

And smiled the brightest smile with the softest glow
Thank you, Divine Spirit for answering my prayers
As I yelled for everyone to come rushing down the stairs
They were overjoyed to see that she was back
The price we paid was worth every dime, in fact
The doctor gave her a clean bill of health, said she'd
        be just fine
I let out sighs of relief and started to cry
I missed her so much for all those years
Now all I'm doing is crying happy tears
I never want to go back to those days
When darkness rolled in and decided to stay

Your Warning

Trapped in a prison I did not build
Trapped behind bars made of blades and steel
You think you're thrifty, and I would not catch on
You smile with a smirk, sitting up there on your throne
Rest assured, I'm smarter than you think
It won't take me long to escape this hell of a place
You see, I got weapons that are bigger than I've shown
You call me a basic witch, for this you are mistaken
For I am a chosen one who cannot be forsaken
You are no match for me or the weapons that I wield
For God's mighty power will surely yield
You're a damn demon who's better left to die
And one day, you will be brought to your earthly demise
I will overcome this, you will see
For I am more powerful than you even thought to
    believe
I work my magic in ways you can't explain
But you will have to answer for the mistakes that you
    made
You'll be punished severely, there is no doubt
For underestimating the witch you took for a little
    tiny mouse
The witch that I am is deep and true
So give up trying to bring me to my knees
For you'll never win because God's always got me
Satan can never win against the Mighty One
I am covered by the one and only Lord from up above

Now the time has come to push or to shove
So crawl back to your cave and leave me alone
Before God rains down hell upon your very own
     blood and stone
If you keep persisting
You'll feel your body crushing like sinew and bone
This is just your warning, take heed if you must
Before I turn you into fire, brimstone, and dust

Addiction

The razor-sharp blade smooth against my skin
Bearing down so gently, let the journey begin
The rake across my skin sends shivers down my spine
A beauty that's endless and as old as time
The first drop of blood starts to rise to the top
The rush I feel deep within
Surrounds me now and flushes my skin
It starts to run down my leg, freeing with it my mind within
The boundaries I've created have now set me free once again
I hunger, I'm yearning, I plea
There's nothing like the rush of blade to skin
Or the power I feel that resides deep within
My heart yearns for yet another slice
I scream out, yet no one hears my cries
This is my addiction, it's sad but it's true
Cutting is a part of me, like breathing is to you
There's no turning back now, you see
There lives a monster inside of me
It's always going to be with me no matter where I go
I have accepted it, yet nobody else knows
It'll eventually cost me my life one day
I'll bleed out and never feel any more pain
But until then I'll settle for this
The magic it creates when the blade touches my skin

About the Author

Luna Nightwolf is a forty-three-year-old woman who embarked on her spiritual journey three years ago. Luna was led by God to tell part of her story in hopes to help other people in their own lives. To show them that someone else has been through what they are going through and made it out the other side. Luna gives all the glory to God. Luna hopes her story gives readers strength and hope to keep fighting and pushing forward knowing there is light at the end of the tunnel no matter how dark it gets. Luna Nightwolf currently works in law enforcement, a role through which she protects and serves her community. Luna also has three sons (ages twenty-four, nineteen, and sixteen). Luna is very family-oriented and spends as much time with them as possible. Luna is very spiritual and has a very close connection with God as well. She is grateful for her many blessings and thankful for all the Almighty has done for her, and she hopes to follow the path he has set her on, which is to help others. Blessed be!

www.ingramcontent.com/pod-product-compliance
Lightning Source LLC
Chambersburg PA
CBHW021133130726
47988CB00003B/1286